Investing

Acquire Knowledge About Stocks, Bonds, And ETFS To
Generate Profits Through Investments In Residential
Properties, And Master The Art Of Achieving Your
Desired Outcomes

Pascal Jiang

TABLE OF CONTENT

Get Cash By Pulling Money Out Of The Property

You're ready to purchase your first investment property once your house has gained value. You should have been looking at areas to buy another property while you have been receiving value through appreciation, value pay down, or raising the worth of your own. You should have enough cash on hand to cover the first investment and stores before you sign a contract. There are three ways to convert this amount to cash:

1

1) A refinance with a "cash out"

2) An extension of the home value credit (HELOC).

3) Get your house sold.

Renegotiating your house will undoubtedly be the best course of action if loan costs have decreased since you purchased it. You should replace your current second home loan with a larger one or maintain your current low-interest first home loan in place and add a subsequent one, assuming that loan costs have increased. You can sell your house and, if you're ready to cash out, buy a venture property and another house at the same time.

Should one engage in the act of selling or refrain from doing so?

You may inquire as to why I illustrated that selling your house was one of the three options to obtain cash. Why not retain it and acquire a larger one instead? While this option may appear satisfactory, it is imperative that you carefully contemplate many factors before proceeding.

Firstly, does the current property you possess generate a favourable cash flow? In the following section, I will thoroughly analyse this matter. However, it is worth noting that when the price of a house increases, it becomes increasingly challenging to rent it out at a rate that adequately covers all expenses.

Furthermore, what is the extent of the value you have accumulated? Without incurring any capital gains tax on the initial $250,000 ($500,000 for married couples). If the value of the property has significantly increased, it may be more advantageous for you to sell the property now, as it would be a tax-free transaction. If you believe that selling the property after three more years will yield a higher profit, you can only access the entire profit if you choose not to defer the gains through a 1031 exchange. If you do that, you will not be able to access the capital because, according to the legislation, it must be invested directly into another property.

If you perform the calculations on income in the subsequent section and determine that your current property will generate additional cash once you withdraw it, you should consider retaining it. You acknowledge that the property possesses a robust attribute and is situated in a respectable locality. Whether you choose to sell your home and use the proceeds to purchase another home or investment property or decide to keep your home as a rental and buy a new home for yourself, the outcome will be the same. The crucial aspect is that at the end of the transaction, you will possess two residences for personal enjoyment and one residence that generates a steady income, thus propelling you towards a prosperous financial future.

Obtaining Your Credit Report

Three distinct consumer credit reporting agencies maintain a record of your loan repayment and generate your credit score once per annum.

The three organisations have established a central website, a supplementary telephone number, and a mailing address for you to request your free 8228 number.

Verifying your FICO evaluation does not have it is wise to monitor it regularly.

You can freely enrol in a service such as CreditKarma.com. You will receive access to exceptionally high scores and reports from two reputable services, TransUnion and Equifax, with weekly updates. In addition, they will also provide you with credit alerts in the event of any substantial modifications to your TransUnion credit report.

Credit Score and Factors Affecting Your Credit

Several variables influence your FICO score. The three most significant factors are your payment history, the total amount and type of your current credit, and the extent to which you are utilising your current credit. If you own a chronically unfavourable payment record, the sole remedy for this predicament is the passage of time. Ensure timely payment of your bills to gradually enhance this aspect of your credit score.

The magnitude and arrangement of your credit are also crucial. Lenders want to observe a certain level of credit history, but having an excessive amount of retail store credit cards might negatively impact your credit score. Finance organisation advances are considered a last resort lending choice and have a greater detrimental impact on your credit score compared to other loans.

The most notable factor, which is also the least modifiable, is that This phenomenon can undergo swift alterations and exert a substantial impact on your credit score.

At the outset, my credit limits and credit cards were charged nearly or up to the maximum amount. Upon settling this debt (specifically $5,000), my credit score improved significantly, transitioning from the mid-600s range to the low-mid 700s range. This enabled me to reap all the advantages associated with a higher credit score, and all I had to do was diligently focus on and manage my existing credit card debt.

The importance of managing your credit card debt cannot be overstated. If your credit card utilisation exceeds 90%, you will face significant penalties. If you possess multiple cards, ensure that you reduce their balances so that no individual card exceeds 90% of its credit limit and that the total amount of your outstanding balances does not exceed 90% of your total available credit.

Prefer to observe that your outstanding debt is 30% or less of your total available credit. Assume that you possess three Visa credit cards and you have an outstanding debt of $5,000. If your total available credit is only $5,000, that appears highly unfavourable. Yo are experiencing extreme pressure, which will result in a decreased FICO score. However, if your overall credit limit amounts to $15,000, and you are utilising only 30% of this credit, it is considered favourable, resulting in a higher credit score.

Methods For Increasing Your Credit Score

Paying your bills on time every time is the most obvious way to improve your financial rating. As previously said, maintaining a credit balance that is closer to zero than your credit breaking point will also improve your FICO score. Control who checks your credit and when by exercising caution. Your score is lowered by about ten points every time a prospective moneylender checks your credit. This might not sound like much, but if a few moneylenders check your credit, it could mean the difference between passing on a deal because you couldn't secure financing and receiving a respectable advance or settling and negotiating.

Furthermore, your credit score will significantly increase, and you will seem like a totally reputable borrower after your cards are fully paid off over time.

Every disclosing organisation has a mechanism in place for you to begin managing a dispute in the event that you discover errors in your report. Strive to seize this opportunity. Finish your job and remove any inaccurate information.

Once more, paying off your debts—including your current credit cards—is the quickest way to improve your credit.

not keeping an eye on your visitors' actions

There are now functional alternatives to surveillance and monitoring equipment. In this game, there are three major players. Party Squasher, Minute, and Noise Aware are among them. Minute is my favourite band, and I actually discovered them. Despite the fact that Noise Aware is arguably the greatest market in the US, they offended me in a direct email exchange after we spoke. I realised I required a device, but it wasn't noise-aware, and the employees of the company, so I started looking for alternatives. I came into this European business that has very little presence in the US. I spoke with them, which is why I began endorsing Minute myself many years ago.

Since then, they've made significant progress, but there are still a few things I find objectionable. For instance, they added a terrible monthly subscription, but they also added some neat features, including the ability to track noise levels. You can select the decibel level of noise that you find comfortable, and it will alert you if it becomes too loud, allowing you to identify instances of disruptive behaviour.

Naturally, the main objective is to stop parties before they start. If you host parties at your house and you weren't in charge of ending them, or you didn't take the appropriate action, like reporting the party to Airbnb for violating your house rules, then the party will continue. If you violate their terms of service and cause a public nuisance, they have the right to prohibit you.

You require surveillance equipment since you're treading carefully. You can respond appropriately if the noise level monitoring equipment indicates that the volume is too high. Furthermore, I don't believe noise-aware has this capability on party squasher and Minute, even if their hardware permits it. However, they can also keep an eye on how many mobile devices—such as Bluetooth-enabled speakers and fancy Wi-Fi gadgets—are present in the house. It's not necessary, in my opinion, as noise levels should be enough to alert you to a problem.

When he makes a noise, you would reply to the guest in a little friendlier manner, saying something like, "Hey, I hope you're enjoying your stay." Please lower the volume as it appears that you are listening to loud music or watching a very loud TV, which is against our quiet hours."

It's a party if you notice a lot of devices and noise starting up. You can approach your guests with even more aggression—like turning it down. When someone violates the property, some security personnel will actually go there and shut it down as well. It goes without saying that you should take that seriously if you want to avoid being banned. Therefore, I prefer the additional redundancies that Party Squasher and Minute have.

I wouldn't say that I enjoy noise-aware since it drills into a socket. Similar to how a light socket is necessary and cannot be removed. It is a very visible device in the wall that is powered by the house. It could be broken off the socket by someone; I've seen it happen.

You can drill minutes on a magnetic plate anyplace. For the most part, it appears to be a smoke detector or alarm. The hardest-to-notice, very nice spots are where you can put it. You can ask your cleaner to take it down, plug it in, and then put it back because it is battery-operated.

The second way for you to be blacklisted has been found. One is stalking your visitors and violating their privacy; the other is failing to keep a close eye on them. Without you taking charge and aggressively intervening to stop them, they are putting on a party. You will be hit by Airbnb on both sides of the issue.

Criminal Past

The third one is really typical. If Airbnb deems your criminal past to be unsavoury, they will prevent you from hosting. People have now contacted me because they hired someone from within their organisation to serve as a co-host. Following their addition to the team, Airbnb ran the individual's information and subsequently blocked those addresses. Consequently, anyone attempting to host at those addresses was also prohibited. Airbnb will link the ban to the account and the concerned address as a precautionary measure against fraud or other illegal activities.

Now, when I picked up the house in Philadelphia, I nearly got kicked out of Airbnb, so things did not go as planned. The landlord was strange, but he didn't tell me anything because he was forbidden. I bought a number of Airbnb houses in the Philadelphia area surrounding COVID-19 because I wanted to buy properties that people would be interested in, and we could write them off and have the money.

A set of townhomes from a property was one of the addresses we were given. They arrived fully furnished, which was my original intention when I decided to purchase pre-equipped homes as they were about to exit the market. The fact that they were barred from another of these residences was not disclosed by the landlord. I, therefore, took them, signed the leases, and turned on the lease. We then attempted to establish listings for them once I received these listings, but they failed to appear. As a result, we nearly ran out of rentals to cover that.

I lodged a complaint with Airbnb, citing our recent move into this house. We are a nationwide firm, and as you can see. However, we are unable to have these actively posted. I was informed in their reply that it was prohibited. I think that's really amazing. What can we do to remedy this, as we did not do anything to warrant the ban? They say, "Send us a copy of your lease, proving that you are new tenants, along with the date it was active." I had to show them my leases in order to rectify the situation where the property was prohibited from being a party house throughout the year.

People were aware that the region had party homes. Thus, as soon as ours was put back on the market, we began to experience party squash issues, which is why we initially began employing a security guard. We frequently had to turn people away from gatherings as a result of that. We survived it and turned into a source of conflict, even though it wasn't enjoyable. We managed to complete that procedure in a formal manner. The good news is that there are active ways to collaborate with Airbnb to stop or undo prohibitions. If your account is banned by Airbnb, you can challenge the ban regardless of whether it is on a property or your account.

I showed my friend in the EU how to solve it. My recommendation to him was to record a video tour of the entire house and point out where the camera was located. As you can see, it wasn't in anyone's line of sight. To enter the living room, you must first pass through this hallway and then this direction. He apologised for not understanding Airbnb's terms of service and informed them, acknowledging that, technically, that is the same room. He argues that he has been a host for a sizable amount of time, that he has taken out the camera, and that he will never use a camera again since he doesn't want to inadvertently break any Airbnb rules while providing a service. He will just be using the minute system as a monitoring tool. I counselled him to clarify and restore his faith in the company.

You are not breaching any rules if you use Airbnb's Minute system. In a way, Minute has teamed up with Airbnb, and Airbnb is sort of advertising Minute. Thus, kids are aware of Minutes and enjoy Minutes. That's a safe one, so maybe that resolves the issue, and he resumes hosting like normal.

Augmented And Virtual Reality

The utilization of information technologies that enable users to "navigate" in a different world that mimics our everyday surroundings is a prerequisite for the idea of virtual reality. An entirely digitally interactive world that combines audio and visual cues to create a truly immersive experience.

Information devices or peripherals, like visors (helmets or simple glasses) for vision, gloves for touch, which can replace a mouse, keyboard, joystick, and other manual input systems, and earphones for hearing, allow users to disconnect from their surroundings and engage with dynamic, three-dimensional virtual worlds that realistically engage all senses.

The action on screen thoroughly engrosses the viewer, who is also interacting in real-time with everything replicated in this made-up, parallel, and realistic universe.

Actually, there are two categories of simulations that fall under the umbrella term "virtual reality": immersive and non-immersive.

Using a sophisticated set of accessories, such as special 3D glasses that provide 360-degree, highly realistic vision, the user in the first scenario is cut off from the outside world, transported into a replicated parallel reality, and fully submerged in it. The end product is content that subverts the conventional view of usage and takes center stage. It is no accident that the sense of sight is regarded as the primary sense; for this reason, all virtual worlds are designed with exceptional visual features, making them viable alternatives to reality.

In contrast, the second scenario involves a user who is in front of a monitor that serves as a window onto a three-dimensional world that he can interact with through special joysticks; naturally, this has a different emotional impact on the subject due to the lack of helmets, goggles, or gloves.

In order to fully benefit from virtual reality, the architecture required for viewing must have certain features, such as a field of view between 100 and 110 degrees, a frame rate (the frequency of images projected per second) between

60 and 120 to avoid jerky vision that can strain the eyes, and a gyroscope that, when combined with an accelerometer and a magnetometer, allows for head tracking—the displacement of the image that precisely follows the movements of the head along the four cardinal.

Everything has been purposefully designed to enable human interaction and virtual reality "living."

For instance, when we hear a noise in the real world, we look in the direction of the source of the sound. This is made possible in virtual reality by two factors: a sophisticated infrared pointing system that reads your eye movement (also known as "eye tracking") and provides depth of field, making the immersion in the virtual environment even more realistic. The professional multi-channel audio system inside the viewer offers the sensation of sounds coming from all directions, and the so-called.

The features that enhance the real environment are what make it called augmented reality.

Augmented reality (AR) depicts the real world enhanced with virtual items or details that enhance or "increase" the experience, whereas virtual reality is an entirely digital environment built by one or more computers or software that imitates actual reality.

Indeed, its foundation lies in the augmentation or assimilation of the external world with computer-generated three-dimensional graphical pictures, which alter the initial setting while leaving open the possibility of interaction.

Thus, augmented reality is essentially the process of converting enormous amounts of data and analytics into pictures or animations, a digital layer that is placed on the real environment through integration.

How does one go about making augmented reality?

While it may not be as immersive as virtual reality, it may be viewed with common devices like smartphones or special screens (like automotive accessories) and does not always require specialized viewers.

How is augmented reality implemented?

A smartphone, tablet, or smart glass with a built-in video camera that has been loaded with augmented reality software is the first step towards creating an augmented reality experience. The program uses computer vision technology to identify objects when the user points the device at them and stares at them by analyzing the way the images flow.

Then, in the same way that a browser downloads a page via its URL, the device gets the object information from the cloud. The main distinction is that instead of appearing on a two-dimensional page that is displayed on a screen, AR information is provided as a

3D experience superimposed on the item.

As a result, the user's perception is partially digital and partially real. This is where we need to explain the overlay principle: the object in the picture is read by the camera, and when it is recognized by the system, it initiates a new channel of communication that seamlessly blends in with reality and adds more precise information about it.

The essential piece of gear for augmented and virtual reality is a headset. Thus, it should come as no surprise that some of the most well-known brands in the conventional IT industry have thrown their weight behind the creation of this gear, which, depending on the model, may be intended for a variety of purposes (gaming and more).

The Mountain View company created the Google Glass brand of smart glasses, which are augmented reality-enabled and allow you to access a variety of information. You can read websites and news online, check social media, view maps and driving directions through Google Maps, take part in video conferences, take pictures and videos, and more—all without using your hands. Google Glass received a somewhat muted reception from regular consumers, possibly as a result of its excessively high price or premature release (officially launching in mid-2014), as well as concerns about privacy protection and usability. As a result, Google took the product off the market, and it has never been seen again, despite some rumors of a relaunch.

Libra is the new digital currency that Facebook needs in order to provide financial support through its unofficial community. The Libra Association hopes to be able to reach billions of customers with this anticipated disruption. The reasoning for this is that while most of today's reality exists outside of the financial system, Libra allows it to access resources and opportunities that were previously unavailable. The potential is clearly enormous, and the kind of partners who have already contributed to the project provide the finest assurance for a stablecoin that will inevitably spark a revolution.

With Libra, you can send an installment via Messenger, WhatsApp, or Facebook, and the customer (or organization) that receives the aggregate can switch over the amount at any time using a steady exchange scale that is based on dollars.

It's the digital currency that Facebook has planned and desired. Why? To "rehash cash," as the Mark Zuckerberg group puts it: "transforming the global economy." People will genuinely wish to continue living better lives as a result. Given that Facebook currently has a vast (and growing) global user base it is true that Libra was introduced as a cryptocurrency that was arguably accepted everywhere, had a much larger customer base than any other cryptocurrency at the time, had a unified group behind it, and had a rapid decline in opportunities.

By definition, Libra is a "stablecoin" in the context of blockchain, which is a virtual currency whose value is actually correlated with that of the US dollar. This takes into account straightforward transactions and isolates the value of cash from the highs and lows that the cryptocurrency market has been supporting for a considerable amount of time. The various cryptocurrencies like Ethereum and Bitcoin. A series of low-volatility resources will guarantee reliability; these represent a type of benchmark value that will allow the valuation to stabilize over time, as was the case with the "best quality level" for traditional currencies.

Due to its widespread use on Facebook, Messenger, and WhatsApp, it is a global currency that users should manage. It can be used to exchange money between people, regulate the exchange of large amounts of value between customers and businesses, and allow transactions using sophisticated platforms.

Because of Libra, it is now possible to transfer small amounts of money to another customer at any time. Once this money has been received, the trade can be completed, or the credit can be used again for other purchases made through the platform or for other services.

The "permissioned" blockchain that powers Libra is capable of authorizing deals only after receiving approval from a series of focal centers. Because of this, Libra is a completely different kind of digital money than Bitcoin (permissionless), which is more restricted than free. The Libra Association actually states that it attempts to operate on a permissionless kind of framework, meaning that it does not include control and approval frameworks. However, as of right now, there isn't a sufficiently quick, secure, and adaptable solution available to provide billions of users with such a solution.

Later on, the mechanical core of Libra might develop into a Distributed Ledger Technology that is roughly as open as one could anticipate and in line with Facebook's goal of creating the most open money in the world.

The non-benefit organization Libra Association, based in Geneva, is the organization that runs the program and its executives. The association's responsibilities include maintaining the reserves that underpin the stablecoin and developing the Libra Blockchain, the technological foundation of cryptocurrencies and a platform that can verify value exchanges and individual digital wallets. The final choice is a crucial one; it is the mission itself. It is possible to imagine a system that guarantees the value, transactions, and reserve funds of users just by having the ability to manage specific stores.

The Incorrect Method For Financing Real Estate

It was beginning to pay off that Dr. Simmons had finally put in the time and effort to create his own clinical act. He had long felt the need to allocate funds to land as an afterthought, and he learned of a monthly gathering that brought together local land financiers to plan and exchange ideas. The expert reasoned that this might be a great place to research land contribution and meet the right people to help him get started. As he made his way around the room, a very knowledgeable and kind older nobleman struck up a conversation with him.

John seemed to be a very well-prepared financial backer, the kind of financial life Dr. Simmons hoped to achieve in the future. John gave a brief overview of his life story, detailing how he went from working in a plant and designing houses as a side project to being a full-time land financier and eventually interacting with Japanese buyers to help them find accommodations. With his $4 million portfolio of investment homes, he was currently unwinding, living the high life, and making a few major arrangements to prevent himself from being overly tired. That evening, they exchanged business cards, and each went on to network with other people.

The specialist ran with John again the next month, and they carried on their previous conversation. Only recently had

John discovered an amazing deal, and that evening, he was shopping for the greatest deal from hard cash moneylenders. John had made it clear that, even though he had the money, he always tried to use OPM (other people's money) as quickly as possible. Dr. Simmons was curious about the rates that hard cash moneylenders moved and was shocked to learn that it was customary to move between 13% and 15% annually in addition to a few rate focuses at first. Since he was receiving much lower rates of return where his money was now sitting at a business home, the specialist quickly offered to be the hard cash moneylender. John explained that Larry, who was on the other side of the room, would do it for 2% upfront and 13% annually; as a result, the specialist offered 2% upfront and 12% annually. After shaking hands, the expert went back home brimming with enthusiasm to close his first sale.

An end lawyer handled the preliminary administrative tasks, and the cycle proceeded flawlessly. John started working on fixing the house after it had been shut down and then registered it for sale. It sold quickly, and the specialist went to the closing office to pick up his cheque for the advance compensation plus his interest about ninety days after the advance began.

The specialist asked if there were any more arrangements similar to this as he was leaving the office, delighted with how easy that arrangement was and how well it went. "Well, I do have another that I could use your assistance on," John remarked. Additionally, while

John was still at the end lawyer's office, additional advanced administrative work was completed and marked, and John was examined by the specialist. Simmons believed he had made a really astute move. Without a day's rest, he was receiving something in exchange for his money.

The problem was that Dr. Simmons didn't take the time to carefully analyze the position of the credit, which is a crucial component of lending money on real estate, because the subsequent loan arrangement transpired so quickly. Unlike the primary arrangement, which secured his funds through a home loan in the principal position, the following arrangement required him to put his credit in a subpar position behind the first mortgage because there was already a first home loan on the property at that time.

Regrettably, John's second advance was not repaid quite as quickly. Furthermore, John continued to come up with an increasing number of excuses as the months passed. He stated that the $4 million from the sale of his portfolio would cover the advance for the specialist. John finally stopped attending the neighborhood enterprise events and stopped responding to Dr. Simmons' communications. Lacking any other options, the expert hired an attorney for desertion to get rid of John.

After the attorney got in touch, Dr. Simmons discovered some crippling information. To begin with, the credit was actually documented against John's primary residence rather than a venture property by any means. Second, and perhaps trickier yet, John had really started a second private cash advance a few days earlier with someone else he had met at that financial supporter club meeting, and it was documented before the specialist's lien. The day the advance was made, everything transpired so quickly that no title search was conducted. As a result, the specialist was genuinely unaware of the many liens against the property and chose not to purchase title protection to safeguard himself in the event that title problems arose. When it was finally discovered, Dr. Simmons owed $150,000 on his first mortgage and $50,000 on his second, all on a house valued at roughly $150,000. He also owed $100,000 on his third mortgage. The specialist's lien was essentially unprotected overall.

Simmons believed he could pursue John since he believed he had important resources to follow, even without the land's insurance to secure his money. He found that John had $4.5 million in credits against a $4 million rental portfolio. John had run out of money.

Ultimately, Dr. Simmons never had his original hypothesis back, and the additional legal fees made it a disastrous experience for him. In the end, John had defrauded a large number of members of that local financial booster club. Even though John created a few personal enemies, he never caused trouble. The weight of having ultimately outwitted John by defrauding numerous people of their money overwhelmed him. His cause of death was heart failure. He unquestionably left behind excellent instances of what NOT to do when giving someone else a loan to invest in land.

Avoid Sprinting the Marathon

Greetings, Ultimate Investing Community! I apologize for missing a week's worth of investing nuggets; I had an odd bicycle event that injured my eyes. This week, I'm back at work to observe the wild journey that the US market is currently taking all of us on. The S&P 500 saw a 9.5% decline on March 12, marking the biggest one-day decline since 1987.

Whenever we discuss investing, we constantly stress the need to have a strategy. And the "investing time frame" is a crucial component of the game plan. How long do you invest for each trade you make? This is crucial because, depending on how long you plan to invest, you will take a different action when looking at the same stock or option!

Let's use Delta Air Lines [DAL] as an example from recently. Recently, Warren Buffett purchased shares of DAL at a lower price since the tourism business was being negatively impacted by the coronavirus. When I asked the community for comments on this, I discovered that various people had varied answers due to the differences in the investing periods.

Technical analysis (TA) can be used, and shorting DAL can be considered if you are considering a short-term trade. (We offer safe shorting ideas for the stock in Ultimate Investing.) Warren Buffett, a long-term investor, said the coronavirus effect may have artificially lowered the price, so if you're one of them, you could choose to buy and hold the company based on the fundamentals. [However, as the COVID situation worsened on June 30, 2020, Warren Buffett really sold out all of his airline shares, believing that the fundamentals for airlines had changed.]

Which course of action is best depends entirely on your investment time frame and strategy; there is no clear-cut solution.

Allow me to compare this to running. When participating in a 100-meter sprint, it's important to focus on your fast-twitch muscle explosiveness, reaction time, and take off. If you are running a 42-kilometer marathon, on the other hand, you should focus on your slow-twitch muscle training, nutrition, and hydration during the race. It's a completely different approach, and you should adjust your training and game plan accordingly. To put it succinctly, "Don't run the marathon and vice versa!"

If you like this sharing, please check it!

#3 Using Your Knowledge In an Emergency

"It is not knowing what to do, it is doing what you know."

It is Tony Robbins who said this. I find it quite relevant to the investment mindset, even if he used it for motivational speaking.

"KNOWING WHAT TO DO": After completing our UI Bootcamp, you have the skills necessary to navigate the stock market successfully. But how many of us can put our knowledge to the test in an emergency situation and just act without hesitation?

"Knowing what to do" is the result of education and practice. "Doing what you know" requires both faith and discipline.

This requires faith—belief in your own capacity for alternative thinking. How may one develop this belief?

It's similar to a newborn learning to walk. You learn and gradually come to believe that you can walk as you take one step at a time and stumble along the way. Similar steps are involved in learning to invest, and you have to "fail" before you can truly enjoy success! Of course, failure is less common on the road when you have mentors and support, but it still happens. When the time comes, we should be able to act on our knowledge without worrying or putting it off if we have discipline and faith. Go over discipline in Chapter 1.

For the next few weeks, invest and trade in this erratic market in a cautious manner. Recall that when it comes to TA, we in UI always adhere to our motto of "observe and respond." So, prepare your fundamental analysis (FA) shopping list! Before things get better, there may be more blood on the streets.

The Basics of Investing

In addition to being a great philosopher and philanthropist, Warren Buffet, often known as the "Godfather of Investing," is without a doubt the world's best investor. Without discussing his investing philosophies and a few key guidelines he has provided to the industry, my articles on the subject would be lacking.

First Rule: Never experience financial loss

Rule No. 2: Always remember Rule No. 1

Although it sounds silly, Warren Buffet must have given this some serious thought if he said it.

It's important to understand that he hasn't necessarily profited from his ventures and never lost money. Even though he lost about $23 billion in the 2008 financial crisis, the five essential guidelines he insisted on following when making investments continue to be highly effective.

First off, a stock is an ownership stake in a company, despite the fact that this may seem obvious.

2. Over time, stocks safeguard against inflation.

3. Rigidity does not equal risk.

The equity markets are notoriously volatile. However, for a consistent investor, the short-term volatility of the stock market is outweighed by its long-term gains.

4. Maintain a multi-decade time frame

Warren Buffet always has the long term in mind, and all of his investing guidelines are based on that idea since they enable you to accept volatility and offer inflation protection.

5. Use index funds and pay attention to fees.

The best investing strategy is indexing. Buffett suggests that you should be cautious about the fees you pay fund managers since, in general, they are more concerned with earning large fees for themselves than with providing returns to their clients. The effect of inflation on share markets

It is often known that inflation destroys people's investments and savings. People will have to spend more on necessities if inflation spirals out of control and rises too high, which will force them to cease purchasing non-essential items. Due to the decline in the demand for various items and the resulting impact on industry earnings, this will cause the economy to stagnate. These companies' stock values will decline as a result of lower earnings. People will have less money to invest due to a number of factors, including the fact that they will be spending more on necessities. The market will have a liquidity crisis as a result, and prices will decline even more.

This is explained quite clearly by Dennis Ferguson's response. When inflation is severe, as it was in the 1970s, firms and consumers lose purchasing power, which in turn reduces investment and consumption. A recession can strike the economy very fast in such a bad environment.

The following basic guidelines allow for some variances.

When Growth and Inflation are High, Resources and Real Estate Perform Best

Growth Stocks Perform in High Growth and Low Inflation

Bonds increase in Low Growth and Low Inflation

Gold performs best in low-growth and high-inflation environments, where most stocks underperform.

Understanding the existing economic system is not difficult. Maintaining the best investments for that regime and refraining from trading them is the more difficult part.

Which part is the hardest? Recognizing the end of a regime and making timely adjustments to the portfolio! A shift of this kind is coming. Changing from poor growth to high inflation to high growth to low inflation!

How to react if the stock market plummets

Regarding this, various hypotheses and viewpoints exist.

Some advise, "Do nothing and remain calm." This doesn't work for me. Being silent and maintaining composure is not an option.

Some advise you to add more equities to your portfolio and rebalance it. Indeed, this is something that can be done, depending on how much you have already invested and how much liquidity remains after taking a look at the state of the markets.

The third theory is having stop losses on all of your shares when the prices fall below the designated level. They also advise selling when signs point to it and only buying when the reverse happens. For investors, this is a bad idea. This stop-loss mechanism benefits traders and investors. This doesn't seem to work too often for me. I've seen that the stock hits another low when it moves below its fifty-hundred-day moving average. They frequently continue to dip below the fifty- or hundred-day moving averages for days or months at a time, then they rise above and then fall below once more. There's a good chance the investor may become perplexed and end up in worse shape.

"You should be greedy when everybody else is fearful," states Warren Buffett. Again, the ability to accurately estimate whether or not everyone else is experiencing dread is a personal assessment.

Some believe that as long as stocks are declining, they should never be purchased. Once more, it's hard to predict when the autumn will end. Often, the price of a specific share will decline as expected, but it will first take a hit and then rise by, say twenty to thirty percent. In my opinion, it is preferable to determine in advance the price at which a person will purchase any specific stock.

Official Schooling Is Not Important

Sort of, anyway. A handful of the things you learn in school will assist you in becoming a land contributor. My academic background was primarily in design, and I can assure you that my strong bookkeeping and math skills have played a significant role in my professional career. However, I am aware of a few successful financial backers who have very little formal education and who accomplish far more incredible things in the nation than I do.

Today is the day, finally, that we realize there are different kinds of virtuosos among people. Previously, failing a math class was regarded as a sign of inexperience, and the student was considered to be unintelligent. Though we now know that virtuoso experts, for example, probably won't be able to pass a math class, that doesn't tell us anything about their actual intelligence. Therefore, performing poorly academically is by no means an indication of your true suitability.

Students who didn't fare as well with the book-shrewd type of learning can not only have many opportunities to succeed in the land, but they also may have a better chance of thriving than someone who only possesses book smarts in an industry like the land where imagination thrives.

It doesn't really matter what kind of training you received in the past if it didn't affect your ability to advance as a financial backer. Furthermore, you won't often be asked to submit a resume in this field, so you shouldn't worry about adding anything extravagant—if anything at all—to the "Schooling" section.

Adaptability

The number of different options for being a land financial backer is almost absurd. For example, if you have ever started looking into becoming a land finance supporter, you have probably encountered information on:

wholesale

properties for rent

turning

tax notes

liens

leasing

syndicates

REITs

acquisitions of land

Investing in mobile homes

investing in self-storage

And that's only the start. The list is endless, and each option has completely different skill sets, risk profiles, work levels, financial requirements, and strategies. Having so many options often makes it more difficult to identify your area of expertise, but the diversity of options is what really draws many people to this field. Land gives you flexibility in your work, but it's also flexible in the ways you can do things.

Suppose, based on the above outline, that you decide to use flipping as your method of land speculation. Within the realm of flipping, there are a million distinct methods to get started:

Concentrate on certain regions or communities.

Concentrate on specific property kinds.

Get your properties through a variety of channels.

Manage contractors or complete the task yourself.

Make the investment with a variety of lending options.

Only take on one property at a time. Alternatively, you can hire a workforce to manage several homes simultaneously.

You can also create a flexible schedule based on how your process is organized. Maybe you only need land contributing to be a side gig in addition to your regular job. Taking everything into account, you might just focus more on reconsidering the work or taking on more moderate hobbies. If you decide to make real estate investment your full-time career, you will need to adjust your strategy and approach to be income-focused because your success will depend on that one source of revenue. You can choose to make your contribution something casual, low-maintenance, regular, or any length of time in between; however, regardless of the amount of time you want to dedicate to land contribution, you can also choose when you work those hours. If you're looking for that amazing deal, you might spend four to six months working on a flip project, but after it's done, you spend a month at home relaxing and traveling before starting your next project. On the other hand, it's possible that when working on a project, you prefer to sleep in and work later in the day rather than getting up at six in the morning and starting early as you would at a regular job.

There are endless layers of flexibility in the land contributing. This connects to what I mentioned before about figuring out what works best for you and what will allow you to maintain your mental stability. There is no valid reason to put yourself under stress by completing an activity you detest, doing it in a manner you detest, or on a schedule you detest when there are so many options for flexibility. There are tried-and-true methods for making progress (as well as tried-and-true ways to be completely disappointed), but there is no set standard for how you should conduct yourself.

Some people will actually find this terrifying. Many people require or require structure. There are ways to be land-contributing without having to rely on adaptation, but land-contributing is a great place to be if you want to live your life the way you want. In my opinion, there isn't an industry that is more flexible than land investing.

Opportunities For Alternative Investments

Through transactions or resource growth over time, you might possess a few resources that can bring you income.

Certain opportunities may present an unusual prospect, while others have the potential to become a reliable source of income.

This could be done because they appreciate in value over time, because they are unique, or because you may have seen a buyer who is willing to pay a substantial sum of money for what you own.

These could be assets you hang onto for a long period because their value will increase with time, or they might be assets you can sell for a profit.

Let's look at the most well-known varieties.

Wine

Well-made wine matures once it is sealed and gets better with time. Fine wine is becoming more and more in demand globally.

There are various types of wine, including white, red, rose, sweet, and sparkling.

You can ask a vendor for advice on where to find real, high-quality wine suitable for speculating. as even wines that aren't particularly well-known are reasonable investments.

You are investing in a resource that is scarcely produced but in high demand globally.

Since the market is uncontrolled, simply buy from set-up shippers to ensure you have the necessary skills.

Gains in the short term have been possible, but your investment should be viewed as medium to long-term. It is generally accepted that five years is the minimum, while eight to ten years is preferable.

Only certain wines will typically appreciate in value, and they will usually be expensive. Never make a purchase from a company that makes cold calls about wine speculation.

Contribute only if you are confident in your abilities or if you know someone who is knowledgeable at handling fine wine.

A wine that is more than 15 years old should only be purchased if you are an experienced consumer, as the risk of fake wine increases with age.

Verify that the wine jugs are a whole set and that they are in their special wooden case.

The benefits of investing in wine:

• Less volatile; • Offers enticing rewards; • Global demand

Negative aspects of investing in wine:

• Insufficient liquidity • The high cost of storing

- High selling commission charge

- False wine

- An uncontrolled marketplace

Venture-grade wine can be bought from vineyards, specialty shops, internet wine trade, face-to-face barters, and online sell-offs.

Goods and Services

Commodity reserves invest in raw materials or necessary rural goods, which are referred to as commodities.

 Product costs are influenced by foreign politics, supply, and demand.

A few benefits of ware reserves for investors are as follows:

• Diversification of portfolios

• Defence against growth. Costs for items will almost always increase as their use grows, making them one of the few unique resources that benefit from inflation.

• Possible financial growth. Product prices increase in response to consumer demand. A product's cost will increase in proportion to its level of popularity, providing the investor with greater rewards.

There are many different types of item reserves, such as:

- Reserves for indexes. These subsidies keep tabs on a list that includes various ware assets.

- Reserves for commodities. These assets are directly placed within the ware asset.

- Wear ETFs based on futures. Invest in contracts with prospects but never buy real physical assets.

Exchanged commodities are often classified into four categories:

- Metals. Copper, platinum, silver, and gold. Gold has historically been a safe investment. The price of gold also increases when there is a popular expansion. It has successfully preserved abundance for a very long time. You have the option of holding coins or bars. There is no right or wrong response. Gold is considered an important component of any venture portfolio since it reduces the risk associated with the remaining investments.

- Vitality. Add petrol, combustible petrol, warming oil, and raw petroleum.

- Meat and livestock

- Farming. Incorporate corn, soybeans, wheat, rice, chocolate, espresso, cotton, and sugar.

One approach for investing resources into products is through a prospective contract. A prospective contract is valid consent to trade a certain ware resource at a foreordained cost at a preset period in the future.

The purchaser of a destiny contract is assuming the commitment to purchase and get the basic item when the fate contract ends. The merchant is assuming the commitment to give and convey the fundamental ware at the agreement's termination date.

Finding Successful Markets

Finding the Drivers of Profit

The number of vacation rentals is growing rapidly as more travellers realise the flexibility, privacy, and security that come with this kind of convenience. In any case, how can you determine which neighbourhood and kind of real estate to invest in? It takes more than just quickly counting the number of rental properties in your area and estimating the rental potential of a listed property.

The excursion rental industry does not offer "one-size-fits-all" solutions. Condos can rent for more money than large estates in some areas, and rates for waterfront and off-water properties can vary significantly. Additionally, trends in the travel industry are subject to regular changes. The creation of a new gathering spot or attraction can spark interest, and if the media picks up on a new trend, a region may temporarily gain national attention.

A Few Key Profit Indicators

From where are the guests arriving?

How do they travel there?

Local events and attractions

The separation between the attractions

The relationship between supply and demand

Year-round or seasonal demand

Zoning laws

The ratio of the sale price to the nightly rate

Rates of occupancy

Events and Attractions in the Area

You have to understand why people travel to a particular area. There are many different things that can generate interest in a space, so understanding these factors should be your first step. Keep in mind that while some places are more diverse and attract visitors for a wide range of reasons, others may have a few clear reasons why people are drawn to them. It's important to focus only on one attraction or activity when visiting areas with a broad range of offerings. Although we will talk more about that in a later section of this book, it's crucial to discuss now.

Why Do Visitors Come?

athletic events

College activities

Meetings

Musical performances

Museums

Amusement parks

coastal communities

urban regions

 Ski resorts

State and National Parks

Outdoor pursuits

The list is endless.

90

There will be a certain distance that an explorer must travel to reach a particular attraction, and that distance may also depend on other locations in the area that they may need to visit. A visitor staying at an Orlando theme park should be located as close as possible to the recreation area, but a traveller visiting different State or National Parks might prefer a more central location.

List all of the attractions that the various types of explorers will need to see, and determine whether or not it would be feasible for your market to exist if they were equally spaced apart.

Periodic or Constant

After you've established what draws explorers to the area, you should be able to tell whether they visit during different seasons or if it's more geared towards one.

Objections related to seasonality are not inherently bad. In fact, the majority of areas—apart from the objections in metropolitan areas—are sporadic. As long as you are prepared for the slow season and the income generated during the peak season exceeds the annual property expenses, many business sectors can sustain having just one hot season.

Typically During peak season, in certain rare locations, the daily rate is significantly higher than the acquisition cost, allowing you to make a substantial profit on the reserved evenings. The daily rate relative to obtaining cost proportion will be lower in areas with less irregularity. I wouldn't worry about occasional properties because I can still make a similar amount of money from them while using them less frequently. With fewer nights scheduled and more opportunities for me to use the property at my discretion, I also generate a comparable salary.

I'll give you a real-life example of this. Let's say you spend $500,000 on a home on a mountain lake. Your best time of year is actually from Memorial Day to Labour Day. Your daily rate is $1,000 per night during the middle of the year, and your property is fully reserved for ninety nights. There is another property in Orlando, Florida, for $500,000 that you might want to look at. It doesn't have nearly the same slow season as the mountain lake property. Either way, it's a more competitive market, and the average daily rate is $500 per night. To earn the same amount of money as you did on the lake property, 180 evenings would need to be reserved. The Orlando property also had twice the mileage of the lake property. Hopefully, it's clear that having an occasional property isn't always a bad thing.

Distinctions And Commonalities Between Swing And Day Trading

To begin, let me ask you a fundamental question: as a day trader, what are you searching for? This is an easy question to answer.

The first thing you need to do is search for stocks that are trending predictably. After that, you have one day to trade them. They don't have to be kept for more than a day. If you buy Amazon (AMZN) stock today, you shouldn't keep it overnight and then sell it the next day. If you keep onto your position, it is no longer considered day trading. We refer to that as swing trading.

It's important for day traders to know the distinction between swing and day trading. In the latter kind of trading, you keep the stocks for a predetermined amount of time—typically one day to a few weeks. If you want to trade in the swing style, you cannot utilize these day-trading-optimal tools and tactics because this is a different type of trading.

Recall that day trading is an enterprise (Rule 2). Though it's a completely different kind of business, swing trading is nonetheless a form of enterprise. Imagine running a network of hamburger restaurants and a meat processing facility.

Although food is a part of both enterprises, they are not the same. They use various market niches, revenue structures, laws, and timelines in their operations. Just because day trading takes place in the stock market does not mean that it is the same as other trading methods.

Experienced day traders exit their positions before the stock market's closing time. A lot of traders engage in both swing and day trading. They are trained to handle the risks associated with these two types of trading, and they are conscious that they are managing two distinct firms.

The method used to select stocks is one of the primary distinctions between swing trading and day trading. Many traders swing trade the same equities rather than day trading them. Swing traders sometimes search for stocks in well-known companies that they are confident will hold their value over the course of a few weeks.

However, you can trade any stock you wish for day trading, even those that are expected to fail. What happens to the equities after the market shuts is of no concern to day traders.

In actuality, a lot of the companies you day trade are actually pretty dangerous to keep overnight because they could lose a significant amount of their value quickly.

You must decide how active you want to be before you start trading. How much time do I have available, and what are my obligations right now? Your decisions on whether to trade every day or buy and hold for a few days or weeks will be influenced by your responses to these questions.

The day traders and the swing traders are the two categories of active traders. The aim of both parties is to profit from deals, whether they are short-term or long-term.

In essence, day trading is a type of trading in which your long or short position is opened and closed within a 24-hour period on the same day. Day traders enter trades for technical, fundamental, or quantitative reasons. Day traders take time to get comfortable with their positions. In contrast, swing trading involves making long-term investments in assets by buying or shorting them and holding them for a few days, weeks, or months. The swing traders do not plan to make trading their full-time career, in contrast to day traders.

Furthermore, swing trading does not require a large amount of capital, whereas day trading adheres to the "pattern day trader rule." Any trader who executes more than four trades in the same security within a five-day period is subject to this restriction. The trader in question is sometimes referred to as a "pattern day trader" due to the fact that their trades account for more than 6% of their overall trading activity within that time frame. On any given trading day, a pattern day trader's account must have a minimum of $25,000 in equity.

Traders by Day

Although day trading has inherent risks, it may also be quite rewarding. A day trader must understand that he could occasionally suffer a 100% loss.

Stop-loss points. The trades need to be extremely accurate and happen quickly. Being available and understanding what is going on in the market at all times is essential for day trading. The assessments must be carried out regularly, even though it does not mean that one should trade daily or routinely. Compared to swing trading, this kind of trading requires more time. All-day labor can be fulfilling, though.

Those with a love for full-time trading and a strong sense of discipline, decisiveness, and diligence are better suited for day trading. A thorough comprehension of charts and technical trading is essential for day traders to succeed. Because day trading may be a demanding and stressful activity, traders must be able to regulate their emotions and remain composed under pressure.

Ralph Manages To Get Past The Challenge

Ralph came to the realization that he had a classmate in high school, George. George was a Building Construction student at Virginia Tech. After Ralph conducted some research, he discovered that George was employed by a major construction company and was reportedly well-paid. George was well-known for being an expert in his field.

 Ralph realized that George was the path around the impediment.

Ralph drew up a plan that detailed all the figures and the possible earnings from collaborating. He asked George to have lunch with him. They made the decision to launch a company, and over the course of 25 years, they developed a real estate development and construction firm that constructed hundreds of homes annually in addition to flats and commercial buildings. The company sold for a price above $200 million. Ralph made contributions to investments that yield high rates of return on investment. Now, Ralph and George each go about their days in a different way.

There are a lot of things Ralph accomplished that you would want to model your business after. He started with finance, which he enjoyed and was good at, and used it to develop into a go-to person and specialist in the field of construction financing. He located George, who was an authority on the specifics and principles of construction that Ralph was not entirely familiar with. George joined him as a partner. George was a master at managing construction workers and subcontractors to bring the architect's plans to life. This is his area of competence. Thus, one could argue that Ralph and George made a perfect pair.

This highlights a crucial guideline for entrepreneurs: Always select someone who is more experienced than you are in the field. When my brother David and I ran the advertising businesses we started and managed, we had to abide by this guideline. I can say with 100% certainty that it was the secret to the success of our companies. We brought in future titans of the industry, such as Don Just, Mike Hughes, and John Adams.

If there is one thing I can advise you to do after reading this book, it would be to surround yourself, if possible, with intelligent people. Make sure they are the most skilled individuals you can draw in and the greatest in their respective industries, at the very least. Avoid turning into a micromanager. If you want to expand your business, you cannot do everything. You have to be willing to relinquish control and let others handle the labor. Employ and support intelligent individuals. Every job is theirs. Give them the chance to work in every department of the company. And offer them rewards for doing a good job at their jobs. Being a business owner who is employed by the company is not what you want. You want your company to operate on its own. A business that you can walk away from for six months and return to find much better is my dream business. Consider how much simpler it would be to sell a company such as this and how much money you could probably make.

Another thing to remember is that your focus and measurements will lead to growth. Additionally, you might reward managers with bonuses for reaching specific targets. Retain as much of the company's stock as you can. To drive them more, you may instead give important staff a share of the profits. You can let go of employees after they have the resources and rewards necessary for them to succeed. This strategy works best for workers who are capable of completing tasks.

This is the basic idea behind what I refer to as "leverage": money and people leverage. To succeed, astute businesses use the knowledge, intelligence, and motivation of others. Another kind of leverage is monetary leverage. This involves investing your money and leveraging other people's funds to expand your business. For instance, you will remember that Ralph profited from borrowing money in addition to utilizing George's building construction experience. He was able to create construction-financing proposals that bank loan officers considered credible by having a thorough understanding of what the banks looked for in construction loans. This allowed him to use other people's money to grow his company.

Employing Companies

Depending on your hobbies and areas of skill, you can be interested in a wide range of enterprises. Let's keep things easy. I'll give an example using plumbing. The typical salary for a plumber is $25 per hour or almost $50,000 annually. There is always a need for plumbers, and this is a fair income. Assume for the moment that you are new to the workforce and that you enjoy this kind of employment. You might work for a plumbing company to get knowledge of the industry. After you have gotten the hang of the business, you may decide to work for yourself and become your own boss. Customers may pay plumbers more than $25 per hour. Homeadvisor.com states that their hourly rates range from $45 to $200. If you're proficient in your field and provide excellent service to your clients, you'll grow your clientele to the point where you'll be able to bring on additional plumbers to help you finish the project.

Making sales calls and promoting the firm could take up some of your time in order to increase revenue. As the company expands, you will be able to hire more plumbers and dispatch them to complete the necessary duties. If you're astute enough, you can charge enough based on going rates to cover the expenses, advertising, support personnel, and salary of a plumber while still turning a healthy profit. Having additional plumbers will increase your revenue.

Similar work can be done in a lot of other domains. An agency that handles advertising uses the same model. These firms can be classified as "staffing businesses" because they employ persons with certain talents, such as copywriting or plumbing, and then "rent" those workers to organizations or individuals in need of those services.

If you decide to go this way, it's crucial to pick a sector of the economy that provides a service you're interested in. It's critical to have an understanding of the industry or to collaborate with someone who does. The next steps are to find candidates, make an offer, promote, get more business, and assign employees to areas where their expertise is most needed. Employing qualified individuals is essential, especially for supervisory roles. Give them the resources and encouragement they require to be successful, then release them. Having more employees will increase your income. It is crucial that your company doesn't rely on you to manage it if you ever want to sell it. It is far preferable to establish an autonomous business, as I have stated. This will increase the appeal of your company to prospective customers.

Both builders and households require plumbers. Graphic design, nursing, and information technology are some other fields that are frequently brought up. Website development, marketing, SEO, janitorial services, landscaping, and website marketing.Electrical Project Management.Technical Assistance.Production of Videos.And advertising, of course.

Additional Methods For Generating A Steady Income

Another choice would be to save aside money for your own business's startup expenses with the goal of eventually paying yourself a salary. However, you won't be able to pay yourself for a long time with most startups.

Putting money into a pension is another tried-and-true method. A pension is a type of financial plan that lets you accumulate money over time, earn interest, and then get regular payments or even a lump sum payout.

Pensions might be difficult to understand. Additionally, they are dull.

What's wrong with dull, though? For investors, investing might be boring as long as it doesn't result in financial loss. If you are bored, you are allowing time to take care of yourself.

My appetite for danger is really great. Which investing techniques are best for me?

You can join a special club if you are a novice investor with a high tolerance for risk.

The club is referred to as "broke"!

You might have to earn money quickly. And you may have concluded that the best place to accomplish it is on the stock market. If so, begin modestly and abide by this straightforward guideline:

never invest money you cannot afford to lose.

Consider adhering to your financial strategy as your second rule if you can manage the first one.

Changing and chopping their strategy is what causes high-risk investors to lose their money. Given the urgency of the situation, this makes sense.

It is actually better to engage in trading as opposed to investing if you want to make money quickly.

Buying and selling assets is known as trading. As we've already discussed, day trading entails doing this multiple times during the day. Foreign currency, or forex, is a popular market for day traders and a lucrative industry.

HOW ACTIVE IS FOREX?

The way foreign exchange, or forex, operates is by placing bets on the variations in value between currency pairs. The spread refers to this variation in pricing. "Pips" are used to measure the spread. There are three risk-defined formats. Minimal risk: two major currencies that are "major pairs" have minimal volatility. "Minor pairs" couple a major currency with a more volatile one, carrying a medium risk. "Exotics" pairs two highly volatile minor currencies.

That's because you can consistently get lucky in forex trading even if you have no prior trading experience. The issue is that you might then feel pressured to trade more frequently and possibly even take a chance on leveraged trading.

If you're set on pursuing a high-risk investing approach, think about:

Digital Money

It's been said that cryptocurrency will rule all financial transactions in the future. Others claim that because they don't produce any money on their own, they are essentially worthless. In any case, the world of cryptocurrency is the Wild West of investing. The level of volatility is insane. Prices in the entire industry can fluctuate by more than 10% in a single day. What's the best plan you have? Invest in a cryptocurrency that is rising quickly and have it ready to sell at any time. This is a bad investment strategy that is almost guaranteed to fail, yet occasionally, things can work out rather well. Alternatively, conduct due diligence, determine which cryptocurrency will see widespread usage in the future, and make a long-term investment. It's likely that you will encounter some frightening moments. However, this is high-risk investing for you.

ICOs

If you have done your homework, there might be a solid reason for you to invest early in the development of a cryptocurrency. However, if the market is uninterested and the cryptocurrency's price plummets soon after launch, everything might go horribly wrong.

IPOs

Purchasing shares that are being offered for the first time by a well-established traditional company is known as investing in an initial public offering (IPO). Theoretically, an initial public offering (IPO) is a smart way to enter the market at the bottom. The unpredictability of IPOs, however, is a problem. Even an established company with strong financial fundamentals and a solid track record might be ignored by the market, which causes its share price to plummet quickly. This is because market sentiment is subject to change. Uber, a software and taxi company, had a disastrous IPO. One of the main issues that novices with initial public offerings (IPOs) face is the media hype that often envelops them, making it challenging to discern the true narrative.

Venture capital

This entails making startup investments. Maybe you could handle this directly. Or you might be able to locate a fund that makes startup investments. In either case, there are tremendous risks involved because the businesses that depend on your venture capital investment could fail very soon. Because the company has the potential to become the next Apple, the potential benefit is also extremely substantial. The large minimum investment that is typically required is one of the main issues with venture capital for novices.

developing markets

Undeveloped nations are waking up economically all over the planet. You may take advantage of times when growth is at its peak if you time it correctly. For instance, from 2010 to 2018, China was a fantastic place to invest. Investing in emerging economies is best accomplished by locating an exchange-traded fund (ETF) that focuses on these markets.

bonds with a high yield

Junk bonds are a common term for high-yield bonds. You may probably surmise why! Issuers of junk bonds are businesses with low credit ratings. They must, therefore, provide greater coupon rates—or interest—on the funds you lend them by purchasing their bond. A trash bond is consequently fantastic because you get high yields if the company does not fail. In the event that the business fails, you will not be paid, and the bond cannot be sold. Investing in a bond fund that focuses on high-yield bonds is one way to diversify your risk in this situation.

Ignore options, currency trading, and day trading. These offer the easiest path to financial disaster for a novice, even one who is willing to take any and all risks.

Various Investments

You should be aware of the benefits and characteristics of each of these investments if you choose to enter the real estate market.

If you are starting from scratch, we will advise you on which investment is best for you in addition to teaching you about the various options accessible to you. Investing in a property that you won't be able to sell or rent out will only result in you losing the money you paid to acquire it.

As we covered in the last chapter, it is imperative that you identify the problems with it and have them fixed.

This will be one of the greatest strategies for you to start making money because you are probably fresh to the real estate market. Additionally, if you don't have a large down payment, this is one of the least risky investments you can make.

As mentioned earlier, you will be getting a house at a lower cost. There is virtually always a problem in these houses that needs to be rectified. You might put the house back on the market and sell it for more money than you originally bought once you've made the necessary repairs and enhanced its value.

It is a very profitable profit plan if the home market is doing well. Older homes and foreclosures will be more popular for house flipping since, as was previously mentioned, investors can purchase these properties at a reduced cost.

Nonetheless, these repairs are occasionally carried out by contractors. Conversely, a more seasoned house flipper can wind up finishing the project alone. Because you won't be paying someone else to fix the house, you will save some money by doing this.

Consequently, the easiest and fastest way for you to make money in real estate will be to flip houses.

Another kind of house flipping is rehab. Most people agree that this investment is the best way for real estate investors to increase their earnings. You purchase properties that need work, make the necessary repairs, and then resell them for a profit.

Because the house's worth has increased and is now greater than both the purchase price and the cost of the renovations, a successful rehabber will turn a profit.

In this field of investment, a knowledgeable rehab real estate investor can generate substantial profits. Investors in rehab facilities typically generate large amounts of money ahead of the market.

Professionals in the field will concur that the most important piece of advice for earning substantial income when working with rehab houses is to refrain from doing repairs yourself. You can't conclude any agreements on selling the property, which is where you make your money when you are the one doing all the renovations.

A rental property is one where the renters live in the home in exchange for the owner receiving a payment from them, typically on a monthly basis.

You will have no other option if you want to help people. You may make money and help others realise their dream of becoming homeowners by renting out property.

When you wish to buy a house for a certain amount of money and within a certain amount of time, you choose this option. The property will be up for sale, but you are under no obligation to buy it if you so want.

The real estate option and the property leasing option will be aligned by the leasing option.

The rental properties will be either commercial—like an apartment building with four or more units—or residential—like single-family houses.

Your monthly payment will cover the interest on the mortgage as well as any necessary upkeep for the property.

Mobile Homes: This will be a fixed-location caravan home. It's not usually a single-family home, but it's similar to a rental property. However, this comes within the category of rental property.

Most people associate real estate with conventional single-family homes, apartment buildings, or even commercial properties. Nonetheless, purchasing a mobile home might be very advantageous.

The population of people who live in mobile homes is large and continues to rise. It is actually the form of housing that is growing the quickest in the nation. Many families find it too expensive to buy or rent a single-family home because of the high rent. Their only chance to acquire a house is a mobile home, though.

Buying mobile homes could improve your income flow with a few little investments. Purchasing a mobile home and then selling it for twice the original cost is a frequent occurrence.

Furthermore, you might finance the purchase and then profit from the monthly interest the buyer will pay you.

For people who are just starting out in the real estate investment market, the assets we have listed are low-risk and perfect.

We will discuss a few assets that are best suited for more seasoned investors in the section that follows. If the investment is something you're considering, this can offer

Acquire the knowledge that is necessary.

Keep up with market developments and financial news, and don't be afraid to modify your financial investment portfolio as necessary. The best line of defence against people who prey on naïve customers in order to make quick money is knowledge. To avoid going overboard when using your credit card, be sure you are aware of your credit limit. It is your duty to remain informed about such information.

Observe Proper Care of Your Items

Everything from cars and lawnmowers to shoes and clothes survives longer when you take proper care of your house and belongings. What if you didn't need to buy shoes and clothes as frequently as you do? You might spend less money by keeping your automobile longer. The secret to saving money is maintenance.

Live Below Your Financial Capacity

It's not as hard as it would appear to adopt a frugal lifestyle by adopting the mentality of getting the most out of life while using less. Many affluent people led frugal lives in order to obtain their money. Being frugal does not imply choosing a minimalist or dumpster-diving lifestyle or engaging in excessive hoarding. Being frugal means making prudent purchases of valuables and taking good care of them.

Seek Professional Guidance

Getting professional financial guidance to educate yourself and help you make wise decisions will help you avoid troubles, even if you haven't started building wealth yet. Numerous trustworthy professionals are there to assist you for free or at a reduced cost; these specialists range from qualified financial counsellors to nonprofit credit counsellingorganisations to your local county extension specialist.

Remain Well

Some employers only allow a certain number of sick days, so when those days are gone, it's a significant loss of revenue. Illnesses and weight issues drive up insurance costs, and poor health can force an early retirement with reduced benefits. While taking care of your health won't make all of your financial issues go away,

Choosing The Proper Investments

The key to becoming a great investor is committing the fewest errors possible. It goes without saying that all investors lose money. On the other hand, those who are able to avoid making grave errors are the most prosperous.

All things considered, learning involves making errors. But there's a distinction to be made between learning to invest via some setbacks and making disastrous errors that could destroy your account.

Let's look at an illustration of this.

Often, investors let their emotions get the better of them. It is, after all, entirely normal for people to become engrossed in their feelings. If we didn't, we wouldn't be human. However, it's critical to control your emotions, especially if you're having a cold streak.

When they are losing money on a trade, some investors let their emotions get the better of them. Investors frequently decide to stay in for much too long in the expectation that they would eventually recover their losses. But there comes a point at which you have to just give up and leave.

It is imperative that you bear this in mind each time you make an investment. Should you not intend to remain involved for an extended period, cut your losses as soon as they occur. How long it will take to recoup your losses is unknown, if at all.

Your goals will determine whether you stay involved for the long term or for too long. For example, if you invest in a 401(k), you essentially have to stay in the account until you retire. However, it's advisable to sell an ETF as soon as the market turns bad if you want to buy one that you can liquidate at any moment. Waiting for the market to recover makes no sense. The market may take several weeks, months, or even years to return to your initial position.

When investing in a new company or private equity, for example, it is advisable to exit the investment as soon as you suspect problems. It's one thing to experience growing pains; it's quite another to try to weather a company's financial difficulties. You'll probably sink with the company if you decide to stick with them.

These illustrations highlight the necessity of controlling your emotions. You can't let your feelings control you. You'll simply encounter difficulties if you don't do this. Your only option once you get into problems is to get out of there permanently. You can't count on everything to get better overnight. Though it is highly unlikely, it is certainly feasible. It's actually a lot more likely that bad things will get worse than they get better.

In light of this, let's concentrate on the wise choices you should make about your investments. It will be much simpler for you to get a good night's sleep when you make the proper choices the majority of the time.

Chapter 3: The Finest Five Advantages of Investing in and Owning Investment Real Estate

You may be wondering whether purchasing real estate or making investments is a good idea. Best investment ever! Let's examine the primary justifications for real estate investing. The easiest response is this one. This well-known acronym lists the main advantages of all real estate investments. Investment real estate is, to put it simply, the PERFECT investment. The acronym for IDEAL is as follows: * I for Income, * D for depreciation, * E for expenses, * A for appreciation, and * L for leverage.

The finest investment is real estate. I'll go into detail about each advantage.

I - Earnings

In IDEAL, the "I" stands for Income. (often referred to as revenue; positive cash flow) Does it even bring in money? Your investment property should be generating monthly rent. Even though your investment property will occasionally be empty, it will ultimately bring in money. A lot of novice investors overestimate their investments and neglect to account for all expenses. The monthly cost of the property must be disclosed to the investor upfront. Another name for this is negative cash flow. While this scenario is not ideal, there are several circumstances in which it might be appropriate, which we will cover. All of this depends on the owner's risk appetite and capacity to finance and pay for an asset that generates negative returns. During the boom years, prices were high, and rents did not rise as quickly as investments in residential real estate. Naive buyers assumed that property appreciation would offset the drawbacks of a high-interest mortgage.

It is important to give this issue some thought. For the INCOME part of your IDEAL equation to be realized, you must project a positive cash flow scenario.

In order to ensure that your monthly cash flow is satisfactory, it could be essential to make a larger down payment (and hence a smaller mortgage). To have a consistent flow of Income, it is best to pay off your mortgage entirely. This needs to be a crucial component of any retirement strategy. This will guarantee that, as the primary reason you took on the risk of buying investment property, you won't have to worry about money later on.

D: Depreciation

In IDEAL, the letter "D" represents depreciation. Investment real estate depreciation might be utilized to your advantage tax-wise. What precisely is loss of value? It's a non-cost accounting technique that accounts for the monetary cost of real estate ventures. Here's how it functions: As soon as you drive a new car off the lot, its value has gone down. When it comes to homes for investment, the IRS permits you to deduct this amount from your taxes annually. This is not meant to be interpreted as tax advice or as a lesson in tax policy.

The overall value and the time period (which varies based on the type of property—residential or commercial—determine the depreciation of real estate investment properties). It's possible that you've already gotten a property tax bill. The assessed value of your property is typically split into two groups. One for the worth of the land and another for the building. Your property tax base is the sum of these two values. Only the original value of the structure is deductible from taxes. Since land is typically only appreciated, the IRS will not permit you to depreciate the value of your land. It resembles your car pulling off the lot. The property's structure is getting older and less valuable every year. You can benefit tax-wise from this.

Depreciation is the best way to show off the benefits of this concept. An asset that has a positive cash flow might be changed to one that owes money to the IRS and taxes. This allows you to write off the loss (on paper) against your Income for tax purposes. For those seeking a tax shelter for their real estate holdings, it's a fantastic perk.

Let's take the scenario where you have the ability to depreciate a $500,000 investment property for a residence by $15,000 a year. Assume that you have $1,000 in cash flow each month (i.e., after expenses, you are net-positive $1,000 per month) and that the rental Income from this property brings in $12,000 a year. Your accounting may show that, despite your $12,000 in revenue, $3,000 of the depreciation on that investment property was actually lost on paper. Any potential income taxes you owe lessen this. After accounting for the $15,000 in depreciation, the IRS estimates that this property lost $3,000 in value. There are no taxes on the $3,000 paper loss; instead, you can deduct it from any regular taxable income you receive from your day job. Investment real estate that costs more will be of greater quality tax shelter. Investors gain from this because they can use the depreciation provided by their underlying real property investment to deduct as much from their taxable amount each year as they can.

Although it is frequently overlooked, owning investment real estate has many advantages. The explanation above was not intended to be comprehensive because depreciation can be a complex tax topic. When it comes to depreciation and taxes, be sure to consult a qualified tax counselor.